SEE
KIBWORTH
AND
EAT

TRINA WARD INVITES YOU TO

SEE KIBWORTH AND EAT

A CULINARY TOUR

INSPIRED BY A VERY SPECIAL PLACE AND ITS PEOPLE

t

Troubador Publishing Ltd
9 Priory Business Park
Wistow Road
Kibworth
Leics LE8 0RX, UK
Tel: (+44) 116 279 2299
Fax: (+44) 116 279 2277
Email: books@troubador.co.uk
Web: www.troubador.co.uk

ISBN 978 1 78306 316 1

British Library Cataloguing in Publication Data.
A catalogue record for this book is available from the British Library.

Designed and typeset in 12pt Calibri by Troubador Publishing Ltd, Kibworth, UK
Cover design: Alice Buzzel
Printed in Malta by Gutenberg Press

For Kibworth

INTRODUCTION

My love of cooking, writing and the South Leicestershire village that I had recently moved to, were the ingredients that combined and evolved to become the project, or should I say mission, to write a cookbook about, for and also involving, my new community – Kibworth.

I wanted to do something for my community and liked the idea of raising funds through the sale of this book. The fundraising plan changed and evolved over the three years it took me to complete (I wasn't writing the whole time of course – it just took that long while fitting it in with 'normal' life), but perhaps that wasn't a bad thing, as during that time, myself and a group of friends decided to put on a charity music festival in memory of a very wonderful Kibworth man. This was a huge success, and so to facilitate this we launched the Kibworth Charitable Trust – a grant-making trust to support and enable local community initiatives, groups, organisations and individuals, with locally based community-focused projects, facilities or services. And so to this end, all proceeds from the sale of the book will be going to the Kibworth Charitable Trust.

And so back to *See Kibworth and Eat*. The inspiration for the style of book came from a 1950s cookbook, called *See Rome and Eat*. It is a tour of Rome through its restaurants and their signature dishes. To get the ball rolling I put up notices around the village asking for recipes. It soon became apparent that the contributors felt the same way about Kibworth as I did, as many wonderful recipes and stories came in, including some distinguished contributors; Fiona Cairns, Merton College Oxford and Michael Wood's Maya Vision team all wanted to contribute.

It has been an absolute joy trying all the recipes, researching and writing about this wonderful place. I've learnt so much about Kibworth Harcourt, Kibworth Beauchamp and Smeeton Westerby (we come as a threesome, don't you know). Michael Wood could tell you better than I, but I believe the villages together formed the ancient parish of Kibworth. We are still inextricably linked today through our proximity to each other, our friends, our families, schools and businesses.

The book is very much a team effort, and wouldn't be what it is without our photographer Jerry Wesley, who has been on hand throughout the process to photograph virtually every recipe in here.

So this is a book about a place and its people, told through food – A 'Culinary Tour' if you will. And so without further ado, I invite you to *See Kibworth and Eat!*

CONTENTS

ACKNOWLEDGEMENTS

So many people have given their support to this project – I couldn't have done it without you. Firstly a huge thank you to all the wonderful contributors. I have loved your recipes and your enthusiasm for the project. I hope you enjoy seeing your recipes in print! You are: Douglas Bamber at Merton College, The Story of England Team, Sarah and Lino Poli, Fiona Cairns, Liz Lafford, Jan Ellwood, Julia White, Mary Guildea, Louise Wesley, Erica Parsons, Kate Foster, Caroline Corley, Jill Vickers, Rachael Hill, Gill Guest, Angela Holland, Kibworth Primary School, Kibworth High School, Rob Morton at Bottle Kicking Cider Co, Debbie James and Samantha Scott.

Jerry Wesley – thank you for giving so much of your time to photograph the food. The book wouldn't have been the same without you and your beautiful pictures.

Alice Buzzel – thank you for all your hard work in producing the super front cover and artwork.

Sarah and Lino Poli. You have been an integral part of the book with your amazing recipes, and your support, for both the book and the Kibworth Charitable Trust. I thank you.

Michael Wood and Maya Vision. The Story of England sparked an astonishing interest in little old Kibworth, thanks to you guys. I hope that See Kibworth and Eat can ride the back of your wave and help community projects for some time to come. And thank you to the team for your lovely recipes.

I would also like to give a special mention to Fiona Cairns - for showing your support and contributing the best Victoria Sponge recipe I have ever tasted! You are an incredibly busy person but always seem to find a way to support the community. It really is appreciated.

To Jeremy Thompson and Troubador Publishing Ltd – for your advice and practical support in getting the book to print.

And to my very patient family - Mick, Isabella and Scarlett. Thank you for putting up with, well – everything, and for your honest opinions and support. x

Conversion Charts

Trina says...

I didn't want to 'meddle' with the recipes too much so they remain with the weights and measures as the author dictated. So like me, you might find some of these conversions very useful.

Imperial Weights	Metric Weights
½ oz	10 g
¾ oz	20 g
1 oz	25 g
1½ oz	40 g
2 oz	50 g
2½ oz	60 g
3 oz	75 g
4 oz	110 g
4½ oz	125 g
5 oz	150 g
6 oz	175 g
7 oz	200 g
8 oz	225 g
9 oz	250 g
10 oz	275 g
12 oz	350 g
1 lb	450 g
1 lb 8 oz	700 g
2 lb	900 g
3 lb	1.35 kg

Imperial Volume	Metric Volume
2 fl oz	55 ml
3 fl oz	75 ml
5 fl oz (¼ pint)	150 ml
10 fl oz (½ pint)	275 ml
1 pint	570 ml
1 ¼ pint	725 ml
1 ¾ pint	1 litre
2 pint	1.2 litre
2½ pint	1.5 litre
4 pint	2.25 litres

Please note – if using a fan oven reduce the temperature by 20 degrees.

Gas Mark	°F	°C
1	275°F	140°C
2	300°F	150°C
3	325°F	170°C
4	350°F	180°C
5	375°F	190°C
6	400°F	200°C
7	425°F	220°C
8	450°F	230°C
9	475°F	240°C

MERTON COLLEGE

Through Michael Wood's the 'Story of England' we learnt of the important part Merton College, Oxford played in the development of our village, which started with its purchase of Kibworth from Saer de Harcourt in 1270. This came about because Harcourt, after backing Simon de Montfort in his rebellion against Henry III, was captured at the Battle of Evesham in 1265. He was kept prisoner and eventually pardoned, but on the condition that he sold his lands at Kibworth Harcourt for £400 to Walter de Merton, who was at that time Lord Chancellor of England.

Merton College today still owns land and property in the area, and continues to have strong links with the village. Especially to St. Wilfrid's church. The Warden and Fellows of Merton College took over the patronage of the 13th century church after 1780, meaning that Merton College Fellows were installed as Rectors for the following 150 years, until the formation of the Diocese of Leicester in 1926, when the Bishop became joint patron.

Consequently, I wasn't going to pass up this opportunity to ask Merton for a contribution to the book. Merton's domestic bursar, Douglas Bamber, was extremely helpful. He had a word with the college chef and came back with this gem of a recipe, which I am told, is a favourite of Merton students today. I can see why. This sweet treat is a delight, and was swiftly 'history'!

The wonderful maps of 17th century Kibworth that you see are here by the very kind permission of Maya Vision International Ltd and the Warden and Fellows of Merton College, Oxford.

The Church well

THE

FEILD

Cowpasture in Debdale

26 — 0 — 30

Half Bauke in Debdale

Bush

THE WESTE

on this side f acre : 294-3-06.

FEILDE

2 — 0 — 12.

1-3-36

George

The Scale of Per^s.

BEAVCHAMP.

16   32   48   64

Kibworth 1635

RTH

Owldmill hills

CARLTON Lordſhip

THE EASTE FEILDE

:172-0-14:

TVRLAN

LORDS

M.ʳ Raᵐ Mall

Church Bridge

EASTE FEILDE

:189-0-20:

:54-0-22:

: Eaſte.

Student Lunch Apple Cake

From Douglas Bamber – Domestic Bursar at Merton College

Cake
400g peeled sliced apples – about 1/4 cm thick slices (Merton use Cox's)
3 eggs
250g caster sugar
320g butter
320g plain flour
55g shelled walnuts
40g soft brown sugar
40g sultanas
5g mixed spice
3g ground ginger
1 small lemon – juice

Topping
75g caster sugar
25ml milk
15g butter

Line a square tin with non-stick paper.
Gently melt the butter in a pan and leave to cool down.
Soak the sultanas in the lemon juice and set aside for the moment.

Put the walnuts in to a pan, cover with cold water, bring to the boil and as soon as it boils take the nuts out and leave to cool.

Preheat the oven – at Merton we use a fan oven at 140°c.

Beat the eggs and caster sugar together in a mixing bowl.
Add to this the cooled melted butter and the flour.

Spread two-thirds of this mix onto the base of the tin. Scatter over this half the apple slices, all the nuts, brown sugar, sultanas, juice and spices. Cover with the rest of the apples. Spoon the rest of the cake mix over evenly.

Cook it until it is just springy to the touch – ours takes approximately 40 minutes.

Leave it to cool in the tin.

Bring the topping ingredients to the boil and spoon over the cake while both are still warm.

MICHAEL WOOD AND MAYA VISION COME TO KIBWORTH!

In the summer of 2009, posters began to appear on Parish Notice Boards, calling the residents of Kibworth Harcourt, Kibworth Beauchamp and Smeeton Westerby to a meeting about an event called 'The Big Dig'. As it transpired, it was the beginning of an exciting journey for our community, which started with simultaneous archeological digs around these villages, lead by archeological expert and former Time Team presenter, Dr. Carenza Lewis, culminating in a major series for the BBC – The Story of England.

The person behind this adventure was history guru, Michael Wood, and along with his film company, Maya Vision, they spent many months researching, filming and generally delving into the deepest crevices of our community – from its Roman past to present day.

But whilst Michael and his team may be immersed in all things historical, their taste buds are definitely in the present, and to prove it they sent me these wonderful recipes.

Butternut Squash Thai Style Curry

From Sally Thomas – Associate Producer

Sally says...

*I love this recipe – it's quick easy and you can't go wrong!
Perfect for a winter's evening...*

*To save time you can use a ready-made green curry paste
instead of making up your own.*

It serves 4.

1 butternut squash – peeled, deseeded and chopped into 1/2" cubes
1 medium onion – peeled and roughly chopped
500g of in-season vegetables – such as runner beans, broccoli,
cauliflower, potatoes, carrots, late-season courgettes
1 tin coconut milk – or use a block of creamed coconut, dissolved in
300ml warm water
1" piece of fresh root ginger – peeled and roughly chopped
2 cloves garlic – peeled
1" piece of fresh lemongrass – outer leaves removed
1 fresh chilli – or dried equivalent
1/2 teaspoon ground tumeric
1/4 teaspoon salt
juice of 1 lime – optional
30ml oil – e.g. olive oil, sunflower, sesame oil

To make the curry paste, put the onion, garlic, ginger, lemongrass, chilli, tumeric, salt, lime juice (if using) and olive oil in a blender and puree until a smooth paste.

Peel the squash with a potato peeler. Chop off the stalk and flower end. Chop in half and use a spoon to remove the seeds. Chop into 1/2 inch cubes.

Prepare the other vegetables by washing and chopping into quick-to-cook chunks.

Put the paste into a large pan or wok and fry gently, stirring, for 2 minutes. Add the vegetables and stir, to coat them with the paste. Add the coconut milk and mix well.

Cook gently, uncovered for 10-15 minutes or until the vegetables become tender and the sauce has thickened. Stir occasionally, to prevent burning and uneven cooking. Add more water if the sauce gets too dry, before the vegetables are cooked.

Serve with rice.

Yasai Chilli Men

(Inspired by Wagamama's)

From Rebecca Dobbs – Producer

Sauce Ingredients
2 tablespoons vegetable oil
2 finely chopped lemongrass stalks
1 teaspoon grated ginger root
1 chilli – finely chopped
1 onion – finely chopped
2 garlic cloves – peeled and finely chopped
1 tablespoon soy sauce
1/2 teaspoon salt and sugar
1 red pepper – deseeded and finely chopped
1 tablespoon sweet chilli Sauce – shop bought
1 tablespoon tomato ketchup
300ml water

Chilli Men Ingredients
250g Soba noodles
2 tablespoon vegetable oil
firm tofu – cut into approx. 3/4 inch cubes
sliced mushrooms – one large handful
sugar snap peas – one large handful
1 courgette – cut into thin 2 inch long strips
2 carrots – peeled and thinly sliced
2 tomatoes – quartered

First make the Chilli Sauce.
Heat the vegetable oil in a pan.

Add the lemongrass, grated ginger root, chilli, onion, garlic, salt, sugar, and soy sauce.

Saute for about 10 minutes.
Add the red pepper and cook for another 10 minutes.

Then add the sweet chilli sauce, ketchup and water.

Bring to the boil and let simmer for 10 minutes. Put in a blender.

This will keep for a few days in the fridge.

Cook the noodles according to the pack instructions. Once cooked, drain, cool in cold water, drain again, and set aside.

Heat the vegetable oil in a wok. Add the cubes of tofu and saute until golden. Then add – the mushrooms, sugar snap peas, courgette, carrots and tomatoes. Stir fry till tender.

Add 300ml of the chilli sauce (you'll use all that you made earlier) and bring to the boil.

Pour over the noodles.
Eat!

Trina says...

*Soba noodles are buckwheat noodles. I found them in larger **supermarkets but if you are struggling to find them then use thick,** dried, noodles instead.*

Nicola's Chocolate Brownies

From James Evans – Researcher

100g butter
75g chocolate – the good stuff – 70% cocoa
100g flour
200g caster sugar
1 teaspoon baking powder
3 eggs

Heat your oven to 180°C.

Melt the butter and chocolate together in a pan over a low heat. Keep stirring so it doesn't burn at the bottom. Set to one side.

In a separate bowl, thoroughly mix together the flour, caster sugar, baking powder and the eggs.

Add the chocolate and butter to the other ingredients and pour into a buttered baking dish.

Cook for 15-20 minutes.

Important not to overcook as they're best a bit squidgy in the middle!

Trina says...

'By Gum – these were good!'

14.

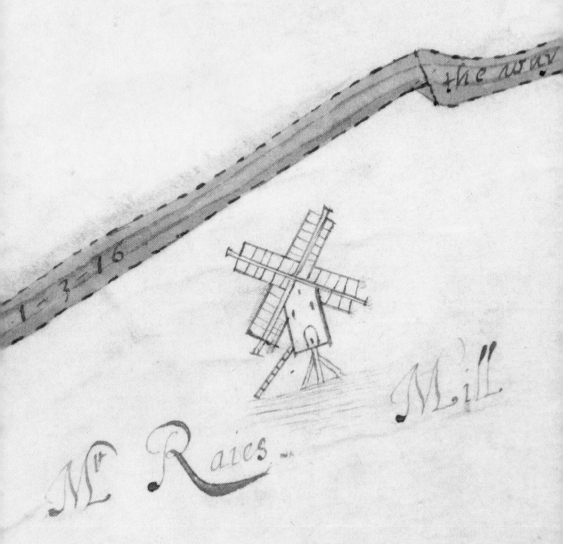

the way

1 - 3 - 16

Mr Raies ... Mill

THE WINDMILL

Head uphill out of Kibworth Harcourt on the Tur Langton road and you will shortly happen upon the Kibworth Windmill. It sits high on a hill looking down over to Kibworth on one side, and to the Welland Valley on the other.

It has for centuries played, quite literally, a 'pivotal' role in the lives of the people of Kibworth. I say 'pivotal' because our windmill is what's called a 'post' mill. The complete wooden structure can, when pushed by the 'tail pole', pivot around a central post in order to turn it into, or away from the wind.

Records show that there has been a windmill in Kibworth from at least 1286, perhaps earlier. In 1286 the mill was owned by Merton College and it was situated on the Carlton Road. It was recorded here again in 1356. But by 1635 records start to show it in its present location on Langton Road. So, not only was it functional, but mobile too. It is written that it was moved with 'wagons and 20 horses or oxen to pull it'. Impressive!

The mill is now under the care of The Society for the Protection of Ancient Buildings, after Merton College gifted it to them in 1936. If you get a chance to visit the mill on one of its Open Days then I thoroughly recommend it. And if you have steady enough legs for the rickety steps and a head for heights, then take a look at the view from the top. It's magnificent.

If a building can have a soul then this one certainly does. The great wooden post through the centre of the mill has been whitened by centuries of flour embedding itself into the grain of the wood. It also bares the carved moniker of millers gone by. Even in its current state of elegant decay I think it is simply beautiful.

Good flour and bread are still in evidence in the village today, and I don't think that anyone knows more about this than Italian born Lino Poli and his wife Sarah. Photographer, Jerry, and I spent some time with Lino and Sarah in the kitchen of their Kibworth Beauchamp restaurant, The Lighthouse (formerly known as Firenze), where Lino was making the day's bread. What a great experience it was to watch a professional handle dough with such confidence and lightness of touch. I will say no more about bread and instead pass this section onto someone with far more knowledge on the subject. Over to you Mrs. Poli....

Il Passione per Il Pane – A Passion For Bread

Italians and bread kind of go hand in hand. It seems to be as much food for the soul as anything, and to generalise about Italian Bread is a mistake to be avoided, as each region embraces its own inimitable style of bread, allowing for the subtle difference that their micro climate, wheat and style of food dictate.

A day without bread is almost worse than a day without sunshine! For us Polis it is no different. As a family we probably eat too much of it. I had almost conquered my craving for it and then Lino started to bake his own at our restaurant, Firenze, in Kibworth Beauchamp. I was doomed...

In 2007 we opened our second restaurant, Boboli, in neighbouring Kibworth Harcourt, and unlike Firenze (now our Lighthouse seafood restaurant) that doesn't serve pizza, Boboli did. And so I had that temptation too – made with authentic Caputo flour!

So our love for the blessed dough continues, increasing weekly with the introduction of our own 'biga', starter dough. So, whilst the mighty, thick, soft, doughy sliced loaf of England has its place, the crunch, texture, aroma and flavour of a good focaccia or pane rustica takes an awful lot of beating.

Lino, and most Italians I know, are quite simply desolate if there is not enough bread at the table. It is a vital part of meal times. Forget this at your peril!

Buon Apetito!

Focaccia

From Lino and Sarah Poli

For the Bread
500 g strong white flour
15g fresh yeast
225g water
2 tablespoons of extra virgin olive oil
10g salt

For the glaze
65 g water
65 g extra virgin olive oil
25 g salt

For the topping

Fresh rosemary sprigs, or olives, pitted ones

Sarah says...

*This Focaccia is as Lino used to prepare when working at the
3 Michelin starred restaurant, L'Enoteca Pinchiorri, where we met.*

Preheat the oven to 220°c/Gas mark 7.

Mix together all the ingredients listed for the bread until they form the dough.
Rub with a little oil and leave to rest for 10 minutes. It is best to cover the
dough with a damp cloth whilst resting.

Oil a baking tray and turn the dough on to it. Rub with a little more oil and leave
for a further 10 minutes.

Using a rolling pin, very lightly roll the dough out from the centre, using the lightest of touches, working the rolling pin upward as it were. It is important for the success of this bread not to batter out the bubbles that are created by the yeast. Leave for a further 20 minutes, and the dough will double in size.

Now, using your finger tips carefully work the dough out, and create dimples in the dough, without breaking through into the mixture. Again, the purpose is to allow the bubbles to be as they are and not battered out.

Whisk together the ingredients for the glaze and pour it over the bread, particularly into the dimples you have created with your finger tips. Leave for a further 20 minutes.

Gently press your topping into the dough and bake for 25–30 minutes until golden brown. Allow to cool on a wire rack

NB: When using the glaze you may need to adjust the quantity of salt. Focaccia is traditionally quite salty, but not always to everyone's taste.

Pane di Polenta

From Lino and Sarah Poli

750g water
300g polenta
600g strong white bread flour
15g fresh yeast
15g fine salt
200g Biga – AKA – "Starter"
60g olive oil

Sarah says...

BIGA – is starter, or mother, and is made using flour, water and something sweet such as fruit. If you are serious about making your own bread it is worth researching and creating your own starter, to have readily available for baking.

Trina says...

I couldn't resist doing my own research on starters, or 'Biga'. It's fascinating. You can see my favourite methods at the end of this recipe. Or research your preferred method on the internet – there's so much information on the subject!

Preheat the oven to 220°c fan/250°c/Gas mark 7-9.

Bring 400g of the water to the boil and add the polenta. Stir well, and beat slowly, so that the mixture is smooth. Cook for a few minutes. Remove from the heat and put in a tray to cool.

Use the remaining water to fix the flour, yeast and starter, in a mixer with a dough hook for 3-4 minutes. Allow the dough to rest for 10-15 minutes before

adding the salt and polenta mixture, then mix for a further 8-10 minutes, on the second speed, the dough should barely be warm after the second mixing.

Oil a deep bowl and turn the dough into it, "dimple" the dough with your finger tips and fold, and leave to rest for 20 minutes. Repeat this procedure again, cut in half, spray with oil and leave for a further 20 minutes.

Shape each piece of dough by stretching, and pulling the dough into the centre, keep doing this until you have a completely smooth ball.

Place both doughs onto oiled trays and leave for 40 minutes until the dough doubles in size.

With a sharp knife cut a cross in the top of the doughs, as they will expand further during baking, then bake for 30–40 minutes, then cool on a wire rack.

Italian Biga

Trina says...

*OK, so there are many methods of making bread starters out there.
Here are two methods I liked because they're not over complicated.
Some pre-planning is required when using a recipe that requires a
'starter' as they need a little time to 'do their thing'.*

Italian Biga – Dried Yeast Method

You'll need
150ml cold water
3g dried yeast
250g very strong flour

Add the yeast to the water and mix well.
Sieve the flour into a bowl. Pour over the liquid and mix well.
Continue to mix for 3 minutes until it forms a dough.

Shape the dough to a ball. Lift it up from the bottom of the bowl and dust underneath it with flour to stop it sticking. Dust the top of the dough too. Cover the bowl with cling film and then a tea towel.

Place the bowl in a cool, dark place and leave to rise for 15 hours.
You can now use your Biga.

Note: do not let it get warmer than 20°C during the raising time as this will cause the yeast to work too quickly.

Italian Biga - Fruit Method

You'll need
1 bunch grapes
250g white bread flour
475ml water

On a board, crush about 300g of grapes slightly. The end of a rolling pin is ideal for this.

Place the grapes in a bowl with the flour and water.
Stir together until the batter has become thick.

Cover the bowl with a teatowel and let it sit at room temperature overnight. The next day, check the starter for bubbles coming to the surface. This is it fermenting. Depending on your environment, this can take up to five days, so please be patient.

Once fermentation starts, strain out the grapes and 'feed' the starter with a bit of flour and water.

You can use the starter straight away or let it sit for a few days longer. However, after four days it might be too sour to use. Your starter need not go to waste though, as it can be frozen in 150g portions to use later.

To bring the starter back to life, let it sit in a glass bowl overnight at room temperature. When the yeasts 'wake up', the fermentation process will start again.

Pizzette

From Lino and Sarah Poli

Base
375g strong white flour
200g water
10g fresh yeast
60g extra virgin olive oil
10g salt

Toppings
Anchovies, tomatoes, garlic olives and mozzarella – whatever
tickles your taste buds really!

Pizzette are great, they are little pizzas really, bite size almost, they make a fabulous start to an evening, or just because you are peckish.

Mix together all the ingredients listed for the Pizzette, except the salt, in a food mixer with a dough hook, for three minutes on the first speed, then add the salt, and mix for a further six minutes on the second speed. At this point the dough should be soft and sticky.

Turn the dough out on to a work surface, clean and free of flour, and using your fingertips, lightly dimple and fold the dough, and leave to rest for 20 minutes.

Lightly flour your work surface and roll out the dough, then cut with a 5-6 cm cutter, place on oiled baking tray and leave in the fridge or cool pantry for 2-4 hours.

Preheat your oven to its highest temperature an hour before you intend to bake the Pizzette, and start thinking about your toppings! Pesto, tapenade, garlic and anchovy paste, fresh tomatoes, mozzarella, parmesan... whatever!

Using your fingertips, prod the dough, working from the centre outwards, and prick with a fork before adding the toppings. Season and bake for 7-10 minutes, until golden brown.

Delicious with a chilled glass of Cataratto!

Panzanella

From Lino and Sarah Poli

Trina says...

What a wonderful recipe this is for a quick lunch. So fresh tasting, and very satisfying at the same time. A win-win situation!

300 g stale bread – preferably Italian bread such as ciabatta
4 tablespoons of white wine vinegar
fresh tomatoes – either 3 large ones or a couple of handfuls of cherry
1 large red onion – diced
1 large bunch of fresh basil
5 tablespoons of extra virgin olive oil
salt and pepper

Sarah says...

This Tuscan bread salad is also as Lino used to prepare when working at the 3 Michelin starred restaurant, L'Enoteca Pinchiorri.

Remove the crusts from the bread, roughly tear it up and soak in the vinegar.

Dice and add the tomatoes to the bread, together with the chopped onion, roughly torn up basil, olive oil and seasoning.

Mix all these ingredients together and serve, either alone or as accompaniment to anything you fancy... griddled steak, fresh sardines, whatever.

Simple, rustic and fabulously good, when the best ingredients are used.

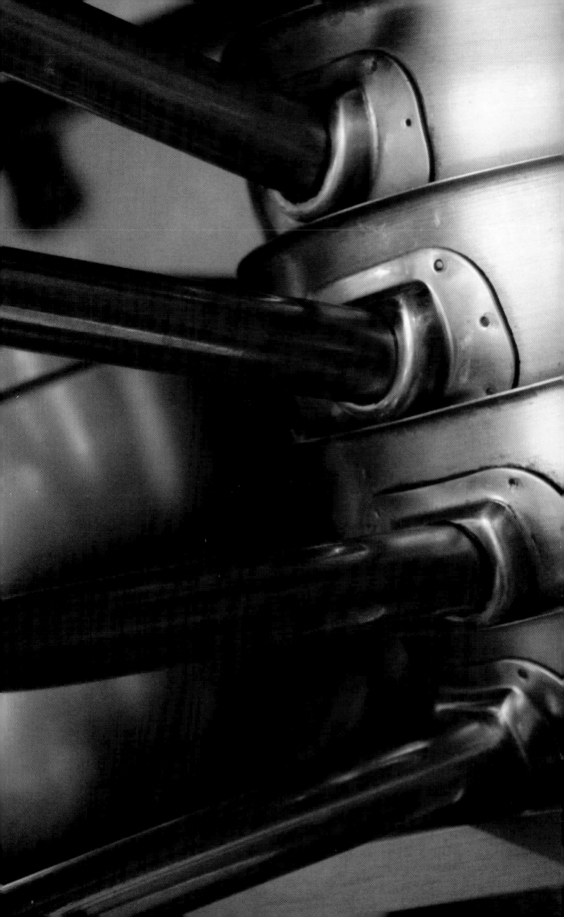

BRIDGE 67 COOKERY SCHOOL

Trina says...

From the tender age of four, cooking with her mother on their sheep and beef farm, Jill Vickers was nurturing her passion for cooking and learning about the best of home-reared produce. She was an early starter in the business world too, when at the age of eight she set up the 'Turner Hen Corporation', selling eggs to friends and family.

This early foray into the food industry was followed into adulthood, as Jill went on to do a degree in BSc Food Marketing and Business Studies. This then took her into the milk and then beer industries. In 2004 Jill went back to farming when she married John, a sheep and beef farmer from Smeeton Westerby. Two children later and wanting to work from home, Jill decided that she wanted to teach people basic cookery skills. And so Bridge 67 Cookery School was born in the farmhouse kitchen. The school has now grown into a thriving business employing three chefs teaching in their new purpose-built cookery school.

As you can imagine, Jill has a large repertoire of dishes, so I have chosen a selection of savoury and sweet dishes that I think you will all enjoy and that do not require too many 'cheffy' skills.

And why Bridge 67? The Grand Union canal runs through the farm and quite simply Bridge No. 67 is their bridge.

Butternut Squash Soup

From Jill Vickers – Bridge 67 Cookery School

1 butternut squash
1 onion
1 potato
1 celery stick
1 carrot
50g butter
600ml chicken or vegetable stock
4 tablespoons cream or crème fraiche
1 tablespoon finely chopped chives

Peel the butternut squash, halve it, scoop out the seeds and cut it into cubes. Similarly dice the onion, potato, celery and carrot.

Melt the butter on a low heat and gently sauté the onion for 10-15 minutes, stirring occasionally to prevent it catching. Add the remaining vegetables and cook for a further two minutes, stirring so everything is well coated in butter. Add the stock and bring to the boil.

For aga cooking, place on the floor of the roasting oven and simmer for 20 minutes, or until the vegetables are soft. For conventional cookers, simmer for 20 minutes or until the vegetables are soft.

Add the salt and pepper. Liquidise and check the seasoning.

Serve the soup with a dollop of cream and some chopped chives.

Creamy Chicken Hotpot

From Jill Vickers - Bridge 67 Cookery School

2 tablespoons olive oil
1kg chicken thigh fillets
3 tablespoons plain flour
1 butternut squash (about 1kg) peeled deseeded and cut into chunks
600g leeks - washed and thickly sliced
750ml hot chicken stock
75g pearl barley
200g pack cream cheese
20g pack flat-leaf parsley - roughly chopped

This hotpot serves six.

Heat the oil in a large pan.

Cut each chicken fillet into 4. Dust in the flour and brown in the hot oil for 4-5 minutes. Add the squash and leeks and cook for a further 2-3 minutes.

Pour in the hot stock and add the barley, bring to the boil, then cover and simmer for about 45 minutes until the sauce has reduced slightly and the barley is tender.

Stir in the cheese, mix until melted, and then add the parsley and season.

Serve with a salad, onion mash and green beans.

Caramelised Red Onion and Gruyere Cheese Quiche

From Jill Vickers – Bridge 67 Cookery School

Pastry
225g plain flour
150g margarine or butter
2 good tablespoons water

Filling
2 large red onions – peeled and sliced
a little caster sugar
4 eggs – beaten
450ml single cream
salt and freshly ground black pepper
200g gruyere cheese – grated

Preheat the oven to 170°c/325°f/Gas mark 3.

First make the pastry – rub the fat into the flour until the mixture resembles fine breadcrumbs. Add the water and work to a firm dough. This can also be done in a food processor.

Grease a 10" (25cm) deepish flan tin and line with the pastry.

If you have an aga, you don't need to prebake and you can now leave to rest in the fridge while preparing the filling.

If you don't have an aga you will need to bake the pastry blind. To do this, cover the pastry with greaseproof paper and fill with baking beans; bake in a preheated oven at 180°c/350°f/Gas mark 4 for 20 minutes.

For the caramelised onions, heat the oil in the pan, add the onions and cook very gently for 20 minutes, without colouring. Add the caster sugar, raise the heat and cook until the onions are caramelised. Spoon over the base.

Whisk the eggs lightly to blend, add the cream and seasoning. Pour over the onions and sprinkle with the cheese. Cook for 30 minutes until set.

For aga cooking, place the flan dish on the floor of the roasting oven and cook for about 30 minutes until golden brown and set. If necessary, turn once to ensure even browning.

Scottish Whisky Tart

From Jill Vickers – Bridge 67 Cookery School

Trina says...

This is an amazing, 'grown ups' dessert – perfect for Sunday lunch.

Pastry
225g plain flour
150g butter – chopped
55g icing sugar
1 egg – beaten
zest of 1 lemon – finely grated

Filling
150g soft dark brown sugar
150g butter
1 1/2 tablespoons golden syrup
3 medium eggs – beaten
zest of 1 lemon – finely grated
150g currants
75g sultanas
75g raisins
3 tablespoons whisky

For the sweet pastry
The best way to make the pastry is in a food processor. To do this, add all the pastry ingredients to the bowl and process until it forms a firm dough. Then turn out and knead lightly before placing in a bag and leave to rest in the fridge for 30 minutes before rolling. Then roll the pastry until it reaches 2–3mm (about 1/8") thick.

Grease and line a 10" flan dish, pressing gently into the edge for a neat finish (leave it untrimmed for now). To blind bake the pastry, preheat the oven to 200°c/400°f/Gas mark 6. Now the top of the edge of the pastry can either be left hanging over during cooking – to trim once baked – or be pressed and trimmed for a 'pinched' finish. Line the pastry with greaseproof paper and fill with baking beans (or rice will do if you don't have beans) and cook for 15-20 minutes. Remove from the oven and lift the paper and beans from the case.

Meanwhile, make the filling

Gently melt the sugar, butter and golden syrup in a saucepan. Remove from the heat, allow to cool and then whisk in the eggs. Stir into this the lemon zest, fruits and whisky until combined.

Pour the fruits mixture into the cooked pastry case and bake 190°c/375°f/ Gas mark 5, for 20-25 minutes. Remove from the oven and leave to relax.

This tart eats well warm or cold – with pouring cream, custard or ice cream.

Chocolate Espresso Fudge Cake

From Jill Vickers – Bridge 67 Cookery School

Jill says...

This also works well with pears, using spices such as cloves, star anise and cinnamon.

Trina says...

This is a cake that brings a smile to your face!

For the cake
85g dark chocolate
60ml espresso
240g plain flour
1 teaspoon baking powder
1/2 teaspoon salt
280g muscovado sugar
250ml sour cream
85g unsalted butter softened
2 eggs

For the Chocolate Fudge Icing
125ml evaporated milk
150g dark chocolate – in pieces
45g unsalted butter – cut into pieces
140g muscovado sugar
32ml espresso

Line a 34.5cm x 24cm tin with greaseproof paper and grease.

Put the chocolate and espresso in a bowl and melt over boiling water.

Sift the flour, baking powder and salt in a bowl. Add the sugar, then add the sour cream and butter and beat with an electric mixer for two minutes. Add the eggs to the batter one at a time, then add the chocolate mix and beat again until combined.

Pour the mix into the tin and slide into the oven for 20-25 minutes at 180°c/350°f/ Gas mark 4. You may need to turn the cake around half way through baking. The top of the cake should spring back when lightly pressed.

Cool the cake in the tin on a cooling rack for 10 minutes, then remove from the tin and finish cooling on the rack

To make the icing, bring the evaporated milk to the boil. Remove from the heat, add the chocolate pieces and let them melt into the milk. Tip the mixture into a food processor and add the butter, sugar and espresso and process until smooth.

Set the icing aside to thicken until it is the desired consistency for spreading. This is a runny icing. Ice the cooled cake with the chocolate fudge icing.

FORAGING FINDS

Kibworth's Harcourt and Beauchamp and Smeeton Westerby are situated in the rolling South Leicestershire countryside, sited in a shallow basin with the hills of Smeeton and Gumley to the south, and the Langtons – a cluster of pretty villages – in the hills to the east. The footpaths that spur off from the villages and across the fields are bordered with lush, thick hedgerows. A ten yard stretch of hedgerow holds within it all manner of culinary possibilities, and since arriving here I have literally picked my way across the fields collecting all manner of edibles.

Elderflower Cordial

From Trina Ward

Elderflower harvesting is incredibly satisfying. Arm yourself with a large carrier bag and a pair of scissors or secateurs. They are best picked just as they are in bloom, usually around the end of May/beginning of June. If the flower heads are going over it can give the cordial a bitter taste.

30 elderflower heads
3 pints boiling water
2lb caster sugar
2oz citric acid – sold in most good chemists
2 oranges – sliced
3 lemons – sliced

Gently rinse over the elderflowers to remove any dirt or little critters.

Pour the boiling water over the sugar in a very large mixing bowl. Stir well and leave to cool.

Add the citric acid, the orange and lemon slices, and then the flowers. Leave in a cool place for 24 hours, stirring occasionally.

Strain through some muslin and transfer to sterilised bottles.

I like to mix with sparkling water, ice and a slice. It is also good mixed with sparkling white wine.

A Note On Sterilising

There are several recipes in this book that require you to sterilise a jar or bottle. Here are a few methods for doing this. Just choose whichever method you prefer and whichever one is most suitable for the type/size of container you are sterilising.

This Is Very Important!
Please note, whichever method you are using make sure you fill your container while the jam or preserve is as hot as the jar (this does not apply to the Sloe Gin). Whatever you do, do NOT add cold food to hot jars, or hot food to cold jars, otherwise the jar will shatter.

In the Oven
Heat the oven to 350°f/180°c/Gas mark 4. No higher or you may risk the glass breaking. Lay a double layer of newspaper on each oven shelf but not the floor of the oven. Arrange the jars on the shelf making sure the jars are not touching each other. Close the oven door and sterilise the jars for a minimum of 20 minutes. Using oven gloves, remove each jar from the oven as needed onto a heatproof surface.

Dishwasher Method
Fill your dishwasher with clean cold jars and run a minimum or rinse wash to time with when your preserve will be ready. Use the jars one at a time from the dishwasher.

In the Microwave
Wash the jars as normal, rinse but leave the jars a little wet. Microwave for no more than one minute on full power.

Sterilising Lids
Wash your lids first. Place them in a pan of boiling water for 10 minutes. Remove them with tongs or a slotted spoon and leave them to dry, underside uppermost, on a clean tea towel.

Slah or 'Sloe' Gin

From Trina Ward

Slah being the old English word for plum, is the fruit of the Blackthorn Bush, or *Prunus Spinosa* to give it its botanical name. Botanical names are very good for giving you clues as to their habit. In the case of the Blackthorn it is quite useful to be armed with this information for your first meeting with this formidable shrub. In botanical speak, *Prunus* means a member of the Plum family, but *Spinosa* means spines. And what savage spines they are too. Leather or gardening gloves are recommended when harvesting this fruit – if you don't want to become perforated...

When picking sloes I feel closer to the past, as I imagine generation after generation of 'Kibworthians' picking their way across the same fields of a crisp, bright autumn morning.

Some say they are best picked after the first frost, usually around October/November. However, I didn't get a look in last year as they had all gone by then. So, if you want sloes guaranteed I would recommend keeping an eye out for them to turn black and plump and go for it. I would also recommend that you only take about 25% from any one bush. A bit for you and a bit for the birdies.

This recipe is to make a 1 litre bottle of sloe gin. You can adjust the sugar quantity based on the sweetness of your tooth.

A 1 litre bottle or jar with airtight sealed lid – with enough room in the neck to push through the sloes
An object for puncturing the sloes, e.g. a cocktail stick, large pin, fork, veg knife
Half a litre of gin – the cheap and cheerful stuff will do very well
Enough sloes to fill the other half litre
150-250g caster sugar, depending on taste

Sterilise your bottles. See section on sterilising on page 45.

Put something good on the radio for this first task. It can be a bit boring (or perhaps therapeutic if you need something mind numbing to do). Prick each individual sloe a couple of times with a sterilised needle, a cocktail stick or cutlery fork, and pop it in the gin bottle. Do this until you've filled half the bottle.

Add the sugar to the sloes. 150g to 250g plus, dependent on the sweetness of your tooth. Now fill up the bottle to the top with gin.

Seal the bottle, give it a good shake, and store in a cool, dry place. You will need to shake your sloe gin once a day for the first week of fermentation. Then once a week for the next 2–3 months. After which time you can strain it through muslin into a clean, sterilised bottle and enjoy.

Nettle Soup

From Trina Ward

One of the tastiest, but slightly hazardous, ingredients to forage for is nettles. I would probably only make nettle soup in early summer as by July the leaves are usually a bit too tough. Nettle soup does freeze quite well though, but leave out the cream until ready to serve.

Nettles - see below for quantity
1 large onion - peeled and sliced
2 cloves of garlic - peeled and halved
2-3 potatoes - peeled and cut into cubes
1 tablespoon olive oil
1 chicken or vegetable stock cube
salt and pepper
cream to taste

Before you start making your soup you will need to pick and prepare your nettles. Unless you like living dangerously, first arm yourself with long sleeves and gloves. Cut enough stems that the leaves from these would fill a large colander.

Rinse the stems under water to clean and rid them of any 'hangers on'. Then with a pair of scissors, cut the leaves off the stems into the large colander. Try not to include any stems. You can leave them in the colander to drain while you prepare the soup.

Place the onion, garlic and potatoes in a large pan with the olive oil.

Stir occasionally over a medium heat until the onion starts to soften. Then add the nettles and stir everything together.

Now add to the pan 1 litre of boiling water and your stock cube of choice. Stir it all together. Simmer for about 15 minutes, or until the potatoes are soft.

Remove from the heat. Allow to cool a little and then 'whizz' in your blender of choice. I like to use a hand-held one so you don't need to decant the ingredients from the pan – saves on the washing up too!

Add salt and pepper to taste.

Now just reheat when you are ready to serve and add a sophisticated swirl of cream to finish.

Gumley Hills

DINNER WITH MRS HILL – YES PLEASE!

Trina says...

Rachael Hill's recipes are ideal for a stress free dinner party. I love the straightforward, no messing style. In fact, very much like Rachael. And with food as good as this, why stress over something complicated? Both recipes are totally delicious and your dinner guests would think themselves lucky to have been invited for dinner!

Rachael says...

This is fab on cold nights or as a winter dinner party.
You'll need to plan a little ahead though as preparation needs to start the previous day.

Lamb Shanks with Redcurrant and Rosemary

From Rachael Hill

4 lamb shanks
2/3 bottle of red wine – remaining 1/3 for the cook!!
handful of fresh rosemary and thyme – can use dried but just a good
pinch of both

2 tablespoons of redcurrant jelly – I have used cranberry to use up after Christmas and it works well
1 onion – chopped
1 carrot – chopped
1/2 pint stock – any will do, I usually use vegetable stock

Put all the ingredients into a large casserole dish. Ensure the meat is fully covered and leave to marinade over night.

Cover and cook at 325°f/170°c/Gas mark 3, for at least two hours – until the meat is tender and falling off the bone.

Serve with mash and seasonal veg.

No Bake Lemon Cheesecake

From Rachael Hill

Base
150g digestive biscuits – crushed
75g butter

Cheesecake Mix
225g plain cottage cheese – works with low or full fat
150ml double cream
50g caster sugar
juice and grated rind of 1 lemon

Melt the butter and mix with the crushed biscuits.

Cover the base of an 8" loose bottom flan dish with the biscuit mix and press down with the back of a spoon. Leave to one side.

Rub the cottage cheese through a sieve into a bowl.

Whip the cream until thick, then fold the cottage cheese, sugar, lemon rind and juice into the cream.

Smear onto the biscuit base and chill for 1 hour before serving.

IN THE GARDEN

If you 'grown your own' you will know the satisfaction that is to be had from nurturing your food from seed to plate. It can be a journey of trial and error, successes and failures, but for me the pleasure of eating your own grown food is well worth this effort; for nothing beats the juicy crunchiness of munching on a freshly pulled carrot, or the creamy white centre of fresh, steaming new potatoes.

It would seem that a good deal of Kibworth and Smeeton residents feel the same. We have a thriving allotment community, with several dotted around the villages. I think that Smeeton Westerby's allotment has to have the best setting though. It forms a kind of island in the centre of the village, with the loveliest whitewashed cottage snuggling into it.

Allotments, vegetable patches and orchards have a lot going for them. They evoke thoughts of a healthy, simpler life; of bygone days, of make-do-and-mend and of community spirit. But for any cook, a patch of fruit or vegetables is also a multitude of possibilities...

Plum Jam

From Trina Ward

There are some amazing fruit trees in the area, especially in the walled gardens of some of the older houses. My personal favourite is the plum. And what better way to enjoy the taste of late summer throughout the winter than to turn the season's bounty into jam. I love this simple recipe from my well worn copy of *Preserving* by Oded Schwartz.

> 1.25kg plums – stoned and halved
> 350ml water
> 1kg preserving or granulated sugar

Have some jam jars ready and sterilised. See section on sterilising (page 45) for methods.

Put the plums and water in a large preserving pan with the water and bring to the boil.

Reduce the heat and simmer for about 25 minutes, stirring occasionally, until the plums are soft.

Add the sugar and stir until dissolved.

Bring back to the boil and boil for about 25–30 minutes.

Test for the setting point. Place a teaspoon full of the jam on a chilled saucer. Leave for a minute and if the jam should 'wrinkle' when you push it gently with your finger, it is done. If not, simmer for another five minutes. Keep doing this until you achieve the 'wrinkle effect'.

Remove the pan from the heat and leave the jam to settle for a few minutes. Pour into hot sterilised jars and seal.

Angela's Tea Loaf

From Angela Holland at Kibworth Garden Centre

Trina says...

And it's not just veggies we like to grow. We also love our flowers. Fortunately for us we have Angela. Angela owns Kibworth Garden Centre, so we can go and see her for our every horticultural need, expert growing advice, and the best Tea Loaf recipe I have ever tasted!

Angela was my first contributor. Talk about starting with a bang – this Tea Loaf is fantastic!

This recipe has come down through generations of the Sanderson family of Kibworth Beauchamp. It was given to Angela from her childhood friend Rosie Sanderson. Angela told me how she loved Mrs. Sanderson's baking. I gather she was the Mary Berry of Kibworth!

Recipes this good and this simple deserve to go on long after us, so I will be sure to pass this on.

And you once you try it, I think you might too.

I love the idea of a 'breakfast' cup. To be honest the size a breakfast cup is a bit of a vexation, so I took a punt and used an average size mug from a well know Swedish furniture store, and it turned out just fine.

1 breakfast cup of cold tea
1 breakfast cup of demerara sugar
12oz sultanas
1 egg – beaten
2 breakfast cups of self raising flour

Soak the fruit and sugar in the tea overnight.

The next day – heat the oven to 180°c/Gas mark 3. Give the fruit and sugar mix a good stir to incorporate any sugar at the bottom of the bowl. Add the flour and the beaten egg.

Butter a loaf tin and pour in your mixture. Cook in the centre of the oven for just about 1 hour.

Take out of the oven and leave it in the tin on a wire rack to cool.

Trina says...

*Turn out and enjoy in thick slices with a large mug of tea.
And if you're feeling totally self-indulgent, spread your slice
with a thick slick of butter.*

Beetroot Jelly

From Gill Guest

Gill says...

This recipe was a favourite of Joyce Wilkinson, my mother's neighbour on Marsh Drive in Kibworth Harcourt. Although Joyce has since passed away, both my mother and sister still make it every year. I regret to say, I don't. I loathe beetroot!

Trina says...

If like me you don't have a pressure cooker – you can prepare the beetroot as per Gill's instructions, place them in a large pan with enough water just to cover. Put a lid on the pan and bring to the boil, then simmer over a medium/low heat, with the lid still on, until beets are tender, about 30-40 minutes depending on size. Peel off skins when they are cool enough to handle.

2 lbs cooked beetroot – see cooking note below
1 pint vinegar
1/2 lb sugar
1oz gelatine – or equivalent for 1 pint of liquid dependent on make/type of gelatine
1 level teaspoon salt

First, to cook the beetroot

Shop-bought, cooked beetroot is not suitable for this recipe as it has not been cooked enough. To cook beetroot for beetroot jelly, wash, snap off leafy tops and use a pressure cooker. Small or medium ones take 15-20 minutes with 1 mug of water, large ones take 30-35 minutes with two large mugs of water. Peel off skins when they are cool enough to handle.

Add the gelatine to the vinegar in a saucepan. Allow to soak, then use gentle heat until the gelatine is dissolved.

Add the sugar and the salt. Stir until clear. Heat but DON'T boil.

Pack beetroot in sterilised jars. Leave small ones whole, slice larger ones.

Pour over gelatine and vinegar mix. Leave to set.

Store in fridge. Lasts for at least a year.

Gill also says...

If you have any leftover vinegar and gelatine mix, add chopped fresh or dried mint to make mint jelly.

MORE RECIPES FROM GILL GUEST

Trina says...

Gill Guest's recipes have been a joy to cook, and I have especially enjoyed the little anecdotes sent with them. When I put the call out for local recipes this was just what I was hoping for. I love a recipe with a tale...

Chicken and Bacon Tetrazzina

From Gill Guest

Gills says...

This is my mother's recipe; Barbara Ward, from Marsh Drive in Kibworth Harcourt. Stock, nutmeg and sherry in the sauce lift this pasta dish out of the ordinary. It's great for using up leftovers of roast chicken and freezes extremely well. Very useful when her children turn up unexpectedly! We can't remember where it came from, but it dates from a time when spaghetti was still something of a novelty.....

6-8 oz spaghetti
8oz streaky bacon
6-8 oz chicken - cooked
1 red pepper
3 oz cheese - grated
1 1/2 oz butter or margarine

1 1/2 oz plain flour
1/4 pint milk
1/4 pint chicken stock
1/4 teaspoon nutmeg
salt and pepper
2 tablespoons sherry
1 oz flaked almonds

Break spaghetti into 4" lengths. Cook according to instruction on pack.

Chop bacon and fry until crisp.

Chop chicken and pepper. Add chicken and pepper to bacon and fry for five minutes.

Melt butter in saucepan. Add flour to the butter and cook over low heat, stirring, for two minutes. Gradually blend in the milk and stock. Cook gently, stirring, until the sauce thickens. Simmer for three minutes. Stir in the grated cheese. Add salt and pepper, nutmeg and sherry.

Put chicken mix and spaghetti in shallow flat ovenproof dish (lasagne dish or similar – mum uses a roasting tin when she's cooking ahead for the freezer). Sprinkle with flaked almonds.

Bake at Gas mark 5 for 25 minutes.

Sausagemeat Pie

From Gill Guest

Gill says...

This is an autumn favourite with all our family, from my mother's next door neighbour on Marsh Drive. The combination of flavours works really well together. It's tasty and unusual.

8 oz short pastry
1 eating apple – peeled, cored and sliced
1 onion
2 tomatoes – skinned
1 lb sausagemeat
a little milk
seasoning

Grease and line an 8" tin with pastry.

Fill with alternate layers of apple, onion and sliced tomato. Season well.

Spread sausagemeat over. Cover with pastry. Brush top with milk.

Cook at Gas mark 7 for 15 minutes then turn down to mark 5 for 40-45 minutes.

Sage and Onion Stuffing

From Gill Guest

Gill says...

This is my grandmother's recipe and therefore probably at least a hundred years old. Catherine Frances Alice Ward lived at Priory Farm on Main Street, Kibworth Harcourt. She didn't use scales. Her cooking involved experience and vague amounts such as "a nob of butter"! In the 1950s, in order to pass her recipes on to her new daughter-in-law (my mother), they worked out the amounts of ingredients that she used and wrote down the weights.

Her stuffing bears no resemblance to commercial packet stuffing. In the twenty-first century, to save time, I make a double quantity and freeze in usable portions. At Christmas, I often defrost a box and combine it with an equal amount of sausagemeat to make 'forcemeat' stuffing.

1 lb onions
4 oz white breadcrumbs
1 teaspoon powdered sage
1 oz margarine or butter
salt and pepper
1 1/2 teaspoons sugar

Peel onions and chop into chunks.

Cover onions with water, boil until very soft (I pressure cook mine for 15 minutes).

Mix the onions with everything and stir together well.

Jamaican Crunch Pie

From Gill Guest

Gill says...

This recipe is delicious but simple to make. It improves with two or three days keeping, so is ideal to make ahead for functions. Good served with raspberries too. This recipe came from my sister, Kate Bish. It is one of my sister's 'O'-level recipes from Robert Smyth School in Market Harborough, given to her during the 1980s by Mrs. Lesley-Miller, who was the cookery teacher there and came from Kibworth.

6 oz ginger nut biscuits – about a packet
2 oz butter or margarine
1/2 pint double cream – whipped
tin condensed milk
grated rind of 2 lemons
12 teaspoons lemon juice

Crush the ginger nuts (put in freezer bag and bash aggressively with rolling pin!).

Melt the butter (or margarine) in a pan. Stir in the crushed biscuits.

Press into base of 9" loose bottomed tin.

Mix the lemon rind and juice into the condensed milk. Fold in the whipped cream. Pour over the base.

Leave to set in fridge for four hours.

MRS WARD LIKES THE SIMPLE LIFE

I don't know about you, but every day seems busier than the previous. This means that my culinary repertoire needs to be quick and simple. I can no longer afford to spend hours over one dish, but I do still want to eat food that is satisfying and tasty. Here are a few dishes that I think do just that.

Miso Soup

From Trina Ward

I find the 'cheats' type jars of ready prepared ginger, chilli, lemon grass, etc., to be invaluable for busy cooks. And it's this type of ingredient that isn't usually fresh to hand when you want to cook something on a whim. I would have no hesitation in using them with this recipe, but obviously you just need to use your common sense when judging the quantity. All I say is – easy on the chilli. You can always add a bit more – much harder to take away!

1 litre chicken stock
2 tablespoons Hoisin sauce
2 tablespoons Oyster sauce
1 tablespoon fish sauce
1 sachet (or 1 large tablespoon Miso) Instant Miso Soup
2" ginger – finely chopped or grated (or 'cheats' ginger)
200g soft noodles – fine or thread work best
1 chilli – deseeded and finely chopped (again, or 'cheats' type)
large or king prawns – cooked – a couple of handfuls should do
stir fry vegetables – a couple of large handfuls. You can use whatever you fancy – mushrooms, beansprouts, pepper, onion, carrot, for instance. Just make sure it is sliced thinly.

Simmer the sauces, miso and ginger in the stock for five minutes.

Add the chilli and vegetables and simmer for a further five minutes.

Finally, add the prawns and noodles. Just simmer these for a couple of minutes as they only want heating through.

Serve in deep bowls and slurp away to your heart's content.

Cider and Spice Ham

From Trina Ward

I find cooking a ham in this way makes for a sticky, juicy meat that melts in your mouth. The amount of spice you use is pretty much up to you – I just chuck in what I feel will give the right balance of flavour – I have given some vague guidelines for you, though.

1 ham joint – raw – I prefer unsmoked for this recipe.
(It is up to you how big as you will be calculating cooking time on weight, everything else is based on volume and the pan you are using)
2 star anise
2 sticks of cinnamon
about 5 cloves
about 8 pepper corns
dry cider – the cheap fizzy stuff will do
water

Place your ham in a large pan – big enough so that the ham is not touching the sides when it's cooking and so that you can place a lid comfortably on the pan – but not so big that you use liquid unnecessarily. Put your spices in the pan.

Pour into the pan the cider until it comes half to three quarters of the way up the ham.

Top up the pan with water until it just covers the ham. Place a lid on the pan and bring to the boil, then turn it down and simmer for about 20 minutes per 450g/1lb of ham weight.

Check the liquid level occasionally and top up with water and/or cider if needed. It is cooked if it shows little resistance when stuck in the centre with a knife, and also if the meat comes easily away with a fork. If testing with a meat thermometer, the internal temperature should be 155°f.

When done, allow the ham to cool in the cooking liquid for several hours.

I don't always bother, but if you want to glaze your ham – remove the skin but leave the about 1/4" of fat in place. Score the fat into little diamond shapes and

brush with a glaze of your choice. You could use honey, a mix of brown sugar and fruit juice or maybe even marmalade! You may also want to push a clove into each diamond.

Bake at 375-400°f for about 15 minutes or until nicely browned.

Scotch Pancakes

From Trina Ward

Scotch Pancakes were a favourite tea time treat for me and my brother. When Mum used to make them we just had them hot, smeared with lashings of butter, so that it dripped down your arm when you ate it. It doesn't get much better than that.

Of course you can have them with whatever you wish. My daughters have them with chocolate spread, I have syrup and fruit, my husband has butter and jam. You can even have them with bacon and eggs.

125g self-raising flour
2 teaspoons sugar
1 egg – beaten
150ml milk
1 tablespoon butter – melted
butter for greasing the pan

In a bowl, mix together the flour and sugar. Then add to this the egg and melted butter. Start mixing this with a whisk and then slowly add the milk, stopping at the runny paste stage to beat out any lumps before continuing to add the remaining milk.

Heat a large frying pan. Once hot add a little knob of butter to grease the bottom of the pan. I use a wad of kitchen towel to help spread it.

Now spoon onto the pan the mixture using a dessert or tablespoon, to make little round pancakes. Don't forget to give them some space so they don't stick to each other. Cook for a couple of minutes until the mix starts to bubble and the underside has turned golden brown. Then turn the pancakes over – I use a palette knife for this, and cook for a further minute until the new underside is golden brown.

Turn out into an ovenproof dish and keep warm in the oven while you repeat the greasing the pan and cooking process to use up your mixture.

Now enjoy with whatever topping tickles your fancy!

NB: If you don't want to cook them all in one go that's not a problem as the mixture keeps in an airtight container in the fridge for a day or two.

Lemon Posset

From Trina Ward

Back in the 90s I used to be the cook at The Bell Inn, Walberswick, a lovely coastal inn in Suffolk. This recipe was given to me by the then landlady's daughter, Verity, which I think she got from another restaurant in Suffolk.

We used to call it Lemon Posset, which I think isn't strictly accurate as in ye olde times a posset was a warmed milk drink, which later became a cooked cream dessert. It should probably have been called a syllabub, but hey ho, it's still damn good. In fact, it's so good that when I returned to The Bell Inn 16 years later, that exact same Lemon Posset was still on the menu!

1/4 glass of white wine
2 tablespoons lemon juice
3 teaspoons grated lemon rind
85g caster sugar
300ml double cream

In a large bowl, or even better, the mixing bowl of an electric mixer, mix everything together but the cream. Add to this the cream and whisk until stiff.

It's as simple as that!

I like to spoon it into wine glasses or dainty little dishes and serve it with a homemade shortbread biscuit on the side to dunk into it.

It usually makes about 6, depending on the size of your serving vessel.

KIBWORTH KIDS LOVE TO COOK!

Hungry Student Stir Fry

From Izzy Ward

Thank you Miss Newington at Kibworth High School! Ever since you taught our daughter this recipe she has wanted to cook and eat it. In fact, she is so deft at it now that when I try and help she tells me to sit down. It serves four so this means I get a night off. That's what I call a result.

dried medium egg noodles – about 3 nests
2 tablespoons oil – groundnut, olive or sunflower are fine
2 carrots – peeled – thinly sliced into about 2" long pieces
1 medium onion – thinly sliced
1 red pepper – deseeded and thinly sliced
120g closed cup mushrooms – sliced
2 handfuls of beansprouts
200g cooked large, king or tiger prawns

For the Marinade
2 cloves of garlic – crushed
3 tablespoons olive oil
1 level teaspoon Chinese Five Spice
3 tablespoons soy sauce

Cook the noodles according to the instructions on the packet. Leave to one side for later.

In a small bowl mix all of the marinade ingredients together and leave to steep.

In a large pan, or better still a wok, heat the oil until shimmering.

Izzy says that Miss Newington likes you to then put vegetables in the pan in the order of 'roots, fruits then shoots'. This basically means add to the pan in order, the onion and carrot, then the pepper and, finally, the mushrooms and beansprouts. Stir fry for a couple of minutes in between each group and then stir fry until all the vegetables are cooked through, but still have a bit of crunch.

Then add the prawns and stir fry until warm. If you over-fry and they'll shrivel up and go hard.

Finally, strain the noodles and add them and the marinade to the pan. Stir fry until everything is coated in the marinade and warmed through.

Serve straight away.

Minted Lamb and Vegetable Meatballs with Herb and Tomato Sauce

From Mandy Lockwood

Trina says...

Whilst our pre-school children may be a bit young for preparing their own meal, they certainly have no aversion to eating well – especially when it's made by Mandy Lockwood!

Mandy says...

When I worked at the Old School Nursery this was one of the many favourite dishes with the children and staff alike. Even the children that were fussy about vegetables loved them as they don't really notice that there's veg in them as it is grated.
Veg by stealth – like it, Mandy!

For the Meatballs

500g minced lamb
1/2 courgette – grated
1/2 carrot – grated
1/2 onion – grated
1 small packet sage and onion stuffing mix
2 tablespoons mint sauce or 1 tablespoon freshly chopped mint
1 egg
salt and pepper – optional to season

For the Sauce

2 400g cans tinned chopped tomatoes
1/2 courgette – grated
1/2 carrot – grated
1/2 onion – grated
1 tablespoon cooking oil
2 tablespoon honey – or sugar to sweeten the sauce
1 garlic clove – crushed
1 tablespoon dried mixed herbs

Preheat oven to Gas mark 5. Bind all of the meatball ingredients together. Leave the stuffing in its dry state – this will soak up the fat from the lamb.

Roll the mixture into small balls, about the size of brussel sprouts. Place in a greased oven proof dish – uncovered, and cook on a middle shelf for 20–25 minutes.

Meanwhile you can start on the tomato sauce. Fry the garlic and vegetables in the oil until soft. Add the tomatoes, honey and herbs. Simmer for about 15 minutes, stirring occasionally.

Add the sauce to the meatballs and serve with pasta or rice.

Mandy says...

If your child is fussy about vegetables then what I do is blitz the sauce in a blender until smooth. They will never know! Enjoy x

Blueberry Muffins

From Kibworth Primary School Cookery Club

Trina says...

The cookery club was set up via a fantastic organisation called 'Let's Get Cooking'. So far there are about 4000 Let's Get Cooking Clubs in England. It is funded by a Big Lottery Fund grant, which pays towards resources, and training. This makes the cookery club very inclusive. The club encourages healthy eating and helps teach the skills that are needed to create simple, tasty dishes.

150g blueberries
250g self-raising flour
140g caster sugar
1 x 5ml spoon bicarbonate of soda
85ml sunflower oil
2 eggs
200 ml semi-skimmed milk
1 x 5ml spoon vanilla extract

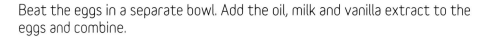

Preheat the oven to 200°c/Gas mark 6.

Put the paper cases into the muffin tin.

Wash the blueberries and leave to drain.

Mix together the dry ingredients in a large bowl.

Beat the eggs in a separate bowl. Add the oil, milk and vanilla extract to the eggs and combine.

Pour the wet ingredients into the dry ingredients and stir until combined.

Fold in the blueberries.

Spoon the mixture into the paper cases and bake for 15–18 minutes in the centre of the oven, until risen and just golden.

Remove from tin and cool a little on a wire rack as best served warm.

Spicy Chicken Fahitas

From Kibworth Primary School Cookery Club

Trina says...

These child-friendly fahitas are not too spicy, but feel free to adjust chilli powder to own taste.

1 red pepper
1/2 teaspoon chilli powder
1/2 small Iceberg lettuce
1 red onion
1 clove garlic
2 skinless chicken breasts
2 x 15ml spoons vegetable oil
1 5ml spoon balsamic vinegar
1 400g can chopped tomatoes
1 x 5ml spoon tomato puree
2 x 5ml spoons dried oregano
freshly ground black pepper
6 flour tortilla wraps
sour cream or low fat crème fraiche to serve

Wash the red pepper and lettuce. Shred the lettuce.

Peel and chop the onion into long thin strips. Cut the red pepper in half, scoop out the insides. Then cut into long thin strips.

Peel and crush the garlic.

With a separate board and knife, slice the chicken into thin strips. Now wash your hands after touching raw chicken.

Heat the oil in a wok or large frying pan. Add the chicken and stir fry for a few minutes until it turns from pink to white all the way through. Add the chilli and stir in for a minute. Add the garlic, onion and pepper and stir fry for a further few minutes, until they start to soften. Add the balsamic vinegar and cook for a few seconds, then add the chopped tomatoes, tomato purée and oregano.

Season with black pepper and cook for about four minutes or until the mixture has thickened.

Heat the tortilla wraps according to instructions on the packet.

Put some chicken mixture in the centre of each tortilla and wrap, adding the sour cream or crème fresh if desired.

Royal Wedding Cake

From Kibworth Primary School Cookery Club

Trina says...

It just so happened that while I was researching this book, Prince William and Catherine Middleton got married. To mark the occasion the Cookery Club made their own version of a chocolate fridge cake that Prince William had requested to be prepared for the wedding banquet. This version is perhaps a little less posh, but, I am sure, no less tasty.

300g Rich Tea biscuits – crushed
170g golden syrup
400g plain chocolate – melted
85g butter – softened
140g raisins

Mix all the ingredients until blended well together.

Pour into a shallow dish and refrigerate overnight.

Whilst still in the dish, cut into suitable sized portions.

Best kept in the fridge to avoid melting.

FIONA CAIRNS

The chocolate fuelled delight that Prince William had requested for his wedding (which was so brilliantly recreated by Kibworth Primary School) was joined by an exquisitely grand confection in the form of an eight tiered rich fruit cake, decorated in elegant cream and white icing, with 900 handmade sugar paste flowers, made by local baker extraordinaire Fiona Cairns.

So, as you can imagine, I was absolutely thrilled when Fiona gave me a recipe for *See Kibworth and Eat*.

Fiona established her business 25 years ago, after making a batch of miniature fruit cakes for friends one Christmas. Her first commercial order was for the Conran shop, and as they say, the rest is history! A barn was converted into a bakery in Fiona and husband Kishore's garden, where a small team of bakers and decorators met orders from Harrods, Selfridges and Fortnum & Mason. In 2001 Kishore joined the company as managing director and the bakery moved out of the garden and into the state-of-the-art bakery in Fleckney. Fiona Cairns now produces over 750,000 cakes per year, including large orders for Waitrose and special orders for celebrities, and of course, Royals.

A good Victoria Sponge recipe is invaluable for the home baker, and the one that Fiona has contributed here is the most consistently successful I have tried; it is light, moist and fabulously spongy!

Victoria Sponge

From Fiona Cairns

Fiona says...

Baking tip to make the perfect sponge – always use the very best ingredients you can, and make sure that all your ingredients are at room temperature before you start. I get my eggs and butter out of the fridge the night before.

For the sponge
175g unsalted butter – really soft, plus more for the tin
175g self-raising flour
1 teaspoon baking powder
3 eggs – lightly beaten
175g golden caster sugar
1 teaspoon vanilla extract

For the Filling
150ml double cream
4 tablespoons raspberry or strawberry jam
icing sugar – to dust

Preheat the oven to 180°c/fan 170°c/350°f/Gas mark 4.

This sponge can be cooked in either 1 x 20cm sandwich tin or in 2 x 20cm sandwich tins. Lightly butter your tin or tins and line the bottoms with backing parchment. If you are using 1 tin then line the sides with a 7cm high collar.

You can use an electric mixer with a beater attachment, food processor or a bowl and an electric whisk to make this batter.

Sift the flour and baking powder into a bowl; add the butter (in knobs), the eggs, sugar and vanilla. Beat together until thoroughly blended to get a light sponge – be careful not to over-mix. Scrape the batter into the tin or tins and level the top.

If you are using two tins then bake in the oven for about 20–25 minutes, or for 30–35 minutes in one tin, until the cake springs back to touch or a skewer inserted into the centre comes out clean. Ovens vary hugely – you will be familiar with yours.

Remove from the oven and leave for a couple of minutes; run a knife around the rim to loosen the cake from the tin and turn out onto a wire rack. Leave to cool down completely.

Whip the cream lightly until thickened to soft peaks. If you have baked the cake in one tin then split it horizontally with a serrated knife. Fill with jam and cream and sandwich together. If baked in two tins, sandwich the two bases of the cakes together.

To finish, dust the top with icing sugar.

Best served on the day.

Trina says...

On photo shoot day I had a punnet of raspberries to play with – they are not compulsory.

BOTTLE KICKING CIDER COMPANY

Rob Morton's journey to commercial cider maker started with a gift of a small cider press from his wife. He used the apples from the Bramley tree in his garden. The results were most pleasing, and his friends would regularly come over and clear him out. Realising he was onto something, he decided to increase production by buying a larger press and bringing in Leicestershire and West Country apples to blend together. West Country apples are high in tannin and so the juice has a big flavour, giving depth and complexity in the final blend. Whereas Leicestershire apples are naturally more acidic, giving a sharpness that beautifully balances the finished brew. And so the Bottle Kicking Cider Co. was born.

Rob and his family live in the pretty village of Hallaton, about nine miles from Kibworth. My first tasting was in Kibworth Wines a few years ago at the village Christmas Shopping Night where it was made into Mulled Cider – more of which later. Rob's company has gone from strength to strength, producing different ciders for different tastes and occasions, and can now be found at many a discerning pub, festival and shop.

So why the name Bottle Kicking, I hear you say? Bottle Kicking is a competition of very few rules – apart from no weapons, strangling or eye gouging – nice! It takes place every Easter Monday on Hare Pie Field – at the back of Rob's house, between teams from Hallaton and Medborne.

To give you the bare bones of the thing, a hare pie is paraded from Medborne, blessed by the vicar, some of it thrown to an assembled mass – this is called a 'scramble'. What is left of the pie is taken, along with three small wooden barrels – aka 'Bottles' – to the top of Hare Pie Bank. The pie is spread on the ground and the bottles are each thrown in the air to signify the start.

The winning team is the one that gets two of the three bottles across their touch line – Hallaton's being the stream which runs along Rob's garden, and Medborne's being the stream one mile away.

It's fierce stuff! I'm sure all involved look forward to a lovely glass of Rob's cider when it's all over.

Rob's Sausages in Draught Scrambler Cider Casserole

From Rob Morton

Trina says...

See Kibworth and Eat's photographer Jerry and I were very kindly invited to Rob's house for lunch to learn about his cider company, sample the cider and try these wonderful recipes that he has created. And what a fantastic lunch it was too. As soon as we entered Rob's kitchen we were salivating at the prospect of lunch, as the sweet, spicy aroma of the mulled wine combined with the fried onions and warm apple smell of the casserole. Food heaven!

650g pork sausages – Rob uses Dickenson and Morris sausages from Melton Mowbray
250g smoked back bacon – chopped
olive oil – enough for frying
300g shallots – peeled and left whole
100g button/closed cup mushrooms – sliced
1 tablespoon plain flour
500ml Draught Scrambler Cider
pinch of rosemary and thyme
1 large bramley apple – de-cored, quartered and thinly sliced
butter – a large knob
pinch of pepper

Brown the sausages in the olive oil in a pan, along with the bacon, mushrooms and whole shallots. Then remove them from the pan with a slotted spoon and place in a casserole dish. Leave to one side.

Add the flour to the pan you've just used and then pour in the cider (do this slowly, stirring continuously so it first forms a paste to lessen the chance of lumps), stirring continuously until it becomes smooth.

Pour the liquid into the casserole dish with the other ingredients and sprinkle in the rosemary and thyme. Throw in a pinch of pepper.

Cover the casserole dish and put into a hot oven – 190°c for 40 minutes.

Whilst this is cooking, fry the slices of apple in some butter until golden brown. Place on top of the casserole for the last 5 minutes of cooking.

Rob says...

We love this served with mashed potato and green beans.

Rob's Scrummy, Scrumpy Mulled Cider

From Rob Morton

3 litres Draught Scrambler Cider
4/5 cinnamon sticks
1 dozen cloves
juice of a whole orange
sugar to taste – approx 6 tablespoons
dash of rum – optional
apple slices to garnish

Combine all the ingredients in a large saucepan.

Simmer for 20–30 minutes.

Ladle into mugs with slices of apple to garnish and serve.

Rob says...

It's delicious with family and friends... especially when it's cold outside!

MARY AND LOUISE

Mary says...

Originally from Bedford, I moved to Leicester in the late 1960s and used to drive past Kibworth every time I went home to see my mum. I thought, one day I am going to live in that nice village. Thirty-three years on and I am still here!

Avgolemono – AKA Mum's Greek Soup

From Mary Guildea and Louise Wesley

Mary says...

My mum used to make this soup for us all – five sisters and two brothers – throughout our childhood, as her mum did for her in Cyprus and I'm sure her grandmother did for her mum.
So long may the recipe be used!

This is a complete meal full of goodness and very tasty! Just writing this reminds me very fondly of mum. x

4 chicken thighs – or a whole chicken (no skin)
1 cup of long grain rice
4 eggs
3 lemons
salt

Cook the chicken in a large pan with enough water to cover it, for about 45 minutes or until the chicken is cooked. Remove the chicken from the pan. Keep the water that remains. Remove any bones and put the chicken aside to add at the end.

To the chicken stock add a cup of long grain rice. Season well with salt and simmer for about 20 minutes. Remove from the heat.

In the meantime, beat the eggs in a bowl large enough to add some of the hot stock later.

Beat the lemon juice into the eggs. A ladle at a time, add the stock and rice to the egg mixture, beating as you do to prevent the eggs from cooking.

Now pour the mixture back into the pan, stir well, add the chicken and serve, adding more lemon juice if required.

Millionaires' Shortbread

From Mary Guildea and Louise Wesley

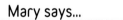

Mary says...

Opening The Deli in the village was a very impulsive decision made after a major operation and needing a project to keep me busy. It certainly did that! After four years of extremely hard work, but lots of fun, meeting some lovely people and enjoying working with my daughter Louise, I am now embarking on the next phase of my life – retirement! And looking forward to it.

This millionaires' shortbread was one of the most popular tray bakes that we introduced along the way... enjoy!

For the Biscuit
8 oz plain flour
6 oz butter – very important to use real butter!
2 oz caster sugar

For the top
1 tin of condensed milk
5 oz soft dark brown sugar
5 oz butter
Large bar of good quality milk chocolate (about 200g)

Preheat the oven to 170°c.

Rub the butter and flour together – to resemble breadcrumbs. Add the sugar, mix well.

Place in a lined tin and press down firmly and evenly with the back of a spoon.

Bake for 12-15 minutes until slightly golden. Remove from the oven and set to one side.

In a large bowl, empty a tin of condensed milk and microwave for a minute or two. Stir well.

Repeat this a couple of times until the mixture is thick, looks like caramel and leaves the sides of the bowl. Remember to stir well after each blast in the microwave. Pour over the cooked shortbread and leave to cool and set.

Finally, break the chocolate into pieces. Place in a bowl and microwave on a medium heat setting – gently, checking after each minute. Pour the chocolate over set caramel and leave to cool.

Just before the chocolate is set, score it into whatever size you prefer – this prevents the chocolate from cracking when you finally cut through it. Yum!

THREE CHEERS FOR COMMUNITY VOLUNTEERS

ERICA PARSONS

Erica is one of those wonderful souls who just wants to make things better for her community. She rarely says no to a request for help, and that is why she has found herself on at least three local committees. All this and she still has time for her family, friends and work. That saying springs to mind, 'if you want something doing – ask a busy person'!

ST. WILFRID'S CHURCH

Once a week the Church Hall at St. Wilfrid's is transformed into a smart café, where the most delicious lunches are served to anyone who wishes to partake.

Like so many community based facilities, it is run by volunteers. And the next few recipes are from some fabulous ladies who volunteer their time at St. Wilfrid's.

Volunteer Jan Ellwood, who like so many of us who have moved into the area, soon discovered that the best way to make friends is to get involved! Volunteering can be very rewarding and a great way to make friends and socialise.

'Three cheers' for community volunteers everywhere!

Golden Chicken Lasagne

From Erica Parsons

Erica says...

This recipe was given to me by my oldest friend Clare, who I have known for over 40 years. She cooked one and brought it along for my big birthday weekend away with eight of my closest girl friends and was enjoyed with plenty of raucous laughter and wine! I have often served it to friends since then and it has always resulted in very clean plates.

It serves about 6 people.

1kg skinless chicken breasts
300ml white wine – half for stock and half for sauce

For the stock to cook the chicken
1 medium onion
trimmings from the leeks – see below
stick of celery
1 bay leaf
6 peppercorns
salt and pepper
water to cover the chicken
200g lasagne – the dried sheets
450g trimmed leeks – sliced
250g mushrooms – sliced
150g butter
1 garlic clove
90g plain flour
90g grated gruyère cheese
50g grated cheddar cheese
300ml single cream
4 level tablespoons grated parmesan cheese
3 level tablespoons pine nuts

Put the stock ingredients in the bottom of a large pan. Put the chicken breasts on top and pour over 150ml of the wine. Top up with water until just covering the chicken and simmer on a low/medium heat until the chicken is cooked through.

Remove the chicken from the pan and cut into bit sized pieces. Strain the remaining liquid into a measuring jug – you'll need this later. Cook the lasagne according to pack instructions if needed (most varieties these days don't require pre-cooking).

Cook the leeks, mushrooms and garlic in 50g of butter in a large pan for about ten minutes. Remove from pan with a slotted spoon and set aside.
In the same pan, add the remaining butter and melt. Stir in the flour and cook, stirring for 1 minute. Take off the heat and whisk in 1 litre of the remaining stock and the remaining 150ml of wine. Bring to the boil and simmer – continually stirring for 4-5 minutes until it begins to thicken.

Take off the heat and stir in 125g (4oz) gruyère cheese, the cheddar cheese, seasoning and cream.

Spoon a little of the sauce into a greased 3 litre (5 1/4 pint) shallow ovenproof dish. Top with a layer of lasagne, followed by half of the chicken, leeks and mushrooms, a sprinkling of parmesan and a little sauce. Continue layering, finishing with lasagne and sauce. Sprinkle over the remaining gruyère, parmesan and pine nuts.

Cook at 200°c for 45-50 minutes.

Leave at room temperature for ten minutes before serving.

Spanish Pork

From Jan Ellwood

Jan says...

I have been involved with the Lunch Stop since 1999, when members of the church decided that we should offer the community a place where they could drop in for a good, reasonably priced meal, a chat and a friendly face.

2lb shoulder of pork – trimmed and cut into bite-sized cubes
2 tablespoons olive oil
1 rounded tablespoon plain flour
2 medium sized onions – sliced
2 cloves of garlic –crushed
1 teaspoon dried basil
1 lb tomatoes – skinned, peeled and chopped or 1 x 400g can chopped tomatoes
6 fl oz red wine
1 green pepper – de-seeded and chopped
2 oz Spanish pimento stuffed olives – sliced
salt and pepper

Pre-heat your oven to 180°c.

Begin by heating the oil in a large flameproof casserole, then add the cubes of pork and brown them on all sides.

Cook only a few cubes at a time and remove them to a plate as they're done.

Add the onion to the casserole and brown them for a few minutes before returning the meat to the pan and sprinkling in the flour.

Stir everything well and add the tomatoes, wine, garlic, basil, salt and pepper. Stir, bring slowly to simmering point then cover with a tight-fitting lid.

Transfer the casserole to the centre shelf of the oven and cook for 1 1/2 hours. After that, add the chopped pepper and sliced olives.

Cover again and cook for a further 30 minutes.

This is delicious served with rice and a crisp green salad.

Battalion Beef Bake

From Julia White at St. Wilfrid's

Trina says...

Julia told me that the bakes are perfect for catering for large, and quite often unknown quantities of people. I'm guessing this dish is so called because making 12-16 portions, it's enough to feed small one – battalion that is!

3 tablespoons corn oil
12oz onions
1 garlic clove – crushed
1 1/2 lb prime collar or slipper of bacon joint, rind removed, cut into 1/2 inch cubes
2 1/2 lb lean minced beef
Juice of a large orange
1 x 14oz tin peeled tomatoes
2 bay leaves
pepper and salt
1/2 teaspoon Worcester sauce
4 lbs potatoes – peeled
2oz butter or margarine
2oz plain flour
1 1/2 pints milk
1 teaspoon mustard
4oz grated cheddar cheese
2 tablespoon grated parmesan cheese

Heat the oil in a large pan and fry the onions and garlic until soft. Add the bacon and cook gently for ten minutes, then stir in the mince. Cook for a further ten minutes, stirring frequently.

Add the orange juice, tomatoes, bay leaves, pepper and Worcester sauce to the meat mixture and bring to the boil. Cover the pan and simmer gently for 45 minutes. Check the seasoning and adjust if necessary.

Cook the potatoes in boiling salted water until almost tender. Drain, cool and slice. Turn the meat mixture into a shallow six pint casserole and arrange the potato slices in an overlapping pattern on the meat.

Melt the butter or margarine in a pan and stir in the flour. Cook for one minute. Gradually stir in the milk and bring to the boil. Add seasoning and the mustard. Simmer for three minutes then remove from the heat and stir in the cheddar cheese. Spoon the sauce over the potato slices and sprinkle with the parmesan cheese.

Cook in hot oven 220°c/425°f/Gas mark 7, for 20 minutes. Reduce the oven temperature to a moderate 180°c/350°f/Gas mark 4, and cook for a further 25 minutes or until really hot and the cheese is brown. Serve immediately.

Blueberry Cake

From Liz Lafford

Liz says...

I did this for an 18th birthday. I dipped some blueberries in icing sugar and sprinkled some with edible glitter... along with sparklers. It was a great celebration cake!

175g soft butter
175g golden caster sugar
3 large eggs
225g self-raising flour
1 teaspoon baking powder
2 teaspoon vanilla extract
142ml carton soured cream
3 x 125g punnets blueberries
200g tub full fat cream cheese
100g icing sugar

Preheat the oven to fan 160°c/Gas mark 4 and butter and line the base of a loose-based 22cm round cake tin with non-stick baking paper or reusable Bake-o-glide.

Put the butter, sugar, eggs, flour, baking powder and vanilla in a bowl. Beat with a wooden spoon for 2–3 minutes, or with a hand electric beater for 1–2 minutes, until lighter in colour and well mixed. Beat in four tablespoons of soured cream, then stir in half the blueberries with a large spoon.

Tip the mixture into the tin and spread it level. Bake for 50 minutes until it is risen, feels firm to the touch and springs back when lightly pressed. Cool for ten minutes, then take out of the tin and peel off the paper or lining. Leave to finish cooling on a wire rack.

To make the frosting, beat the soft cheese with the icing sugar and the remaining soured cream in a bowl until smooth and creamy. Spread over the top of the cooled cake (don't be impatient as the frosting will melt if the cake is too warm) and scatter with the remaining blueberries.

Turkey (or Chicken) and Apricot Bake

From Julia White

1lb turkey or chicken breast – cut into 'stir fry' sized strips
1 oz plain flour
pepper
3 tablespoons olive oil
1 bunch salad onions – chopped
5 oz dried apricots – chopped
1/2 pint milk
3 oz mature cheddar – grated

Topping
1 1/2 oz breadcrumbs
1 oz mature cheese – grated
2 tablespoons chopped parsley

Preheat the oven to 190°c/375°f/Gas mark 5.

Coat the turkey (or chicken) strips in the flour seasoned with pepper.

Heat the oil in a saucepan and cook the turkey for two minutes, stirring continually until sealed. Stir in the onions and apricots and add the milk.

Cook for a further two minutes, stirring until thickened and smooth, then stir in the cheese and transfer the mixture to an ovenproof dish.

Mix together the breadcrumbs, most of the parsley and the remaining cheese and sprinkle over the top. Bake in the preheated oven for 15 minutes.

AND WHERE THERE'S A COMMUNITY EVENT – THERE'S CAKE!

It's amazing, but when and wherever in the community there is a fundraiser, be it a fete, fayre, coffee morning or bizarre, there is also cake. It just seems to appear as if by magic. And no sooner has it been beautifully arranged on a plate – it's gone. Oh yes, you've got to be quick at the olde cake stall in these parts! And my word, Kibworth and Smeeton, you are fantastic bakers!

And to prove it...

Lemon Drizzle Cake

From Erica Parsons

For the sponge
175g unsalted butter – softened
175g self raising flour
175g caster sugar
2 large eggs
a pinch of salt
2 tablespoons milk
finely grated zest and juice of 1 large lemon

For the top
juice of 1 large lemon
100g granulated sugar

Preheat the oven to 180°c/Gas mark 4.

Butter and line a cake tin (square or round – your choice).

Cream together the butter and sugar. Then add the eggs and lemon zest, beating them in well.

Now gently fold in the flour, pinch of salt and milk. Once combined, fold in the lemon juice.

Pour into your prepared tin and bake for about 35 minutes, or until it springs back to touch and a knife inserted into the centre comes out clean.

Meanwhile, make the topping. Very simply, just mix the lemon juice with the sugar.

As soon as the cake is removed from the oven (and still in the tin), puncture it all over with a skewer and pour over the lemon and sugar mix.

Leave to cool in the tin before removing.

Earl Grey Cupcakes

From Kate Foster

Trina says...

The Earl Grey in these cupcakes makes them less sickly and a bit more 'grown up'. You can top them however you wish. I had mine with a simple topping made with icing sugar and water.

2 Earl Grey tea bags
60ml boiling water
80ml milk
100g unsalted butter – softened
2 eggs
150g caster sugar
180g self-raising flour

Preheat the oven to 180°c.

Place 12 muffin cases in a muffin pan.

Place the tea bags in a jug and pour over the boiling water. Make sure they are submerged. Leave for about five minutes. After this time, carefully remove the bags from the water and stir in the milk. Transfer to a large bowl or electric mixer bowl.

Add the butter, eggs, sugar and flour to the tea mixture and beat (on a low speed if using an electric mixer) until combined. Then increase the mixing speed and beat until the mixture is pale and creamy.

Spoon into the cases.

Bake in a preheated oven for about 25 minutes or until golden and a skewer inserted in the centre comes out clean.

Cool on a wire rack.

Flapjack

From Caroline Corley

6oz golden syrup
6oz muscovado sugar
12oz porridge oats
2 tablespoons plain flour

Preheat oven to 150°c/Gas mark 6.

Line an 8" square baking tin with baking paper.

Melt the butter over a medium heat. Add the golden syrup and sugar to the butter.

Once the sugar is dissolved and the butter has melted, remove the pan from the heat and stir in the porridge oats and flour.

Pack the mixture into the baking tin and pop in the oven for 40 minutes.

Happy baking!

THE LIGHTHOUSE

If you've read the Bread, aka 'Windmill' chapter, you will have already made the acquaintance of Sarah and Lino Poli of The Lighthouse – a wonderful seafood restaurant in Kibworth Beauchamp. In their own word's, "There's an emphasis on fish, but plenty to please the meat lovers and vegetarians too. Simple, honest food that warms the soul. The Lighthouse features great British classics and beautifully fresh Mediterranean dishes. Think lobster, potted shrimps, fish and chips. We know you'll love what we're doing. It's food from our hearts." You're not wrong there Mr. and Mrs. P!

Tuscan Fish Broth

From Lino and Sarah Poli

For the stock
2 small onions
2 cloves garlic
2 carrots
1/2 head of celery
seasoning

For the Soup
1.5kg mixed fish and shellfish – look at what is available and go for the
freshest. Include shellfish like prawns, mussels, clams, etc.
2 small onions
1/2 head of celery
2 carrots
425g tin of good plum tomatoes – chop tomatoes and keep juice
1 sachet of saffron
olive oil
15cl white wine
fish stock
fresh basil and parsley

For the stock
Roughly chop the carrots, celery and onions and fry on a gentle heat with the
garlic. Do not brown. Add the shells and bones from the fish and shellfish (see
below). Cover the contents of the pan with water and bring to the boil. Skim the
surface of the 'scum' and simmer for about 20 minutes. Strain and set aside.

For the soup
Clean, scale and fillet the fish. If you ask your fishmonger to do this for you, be
sure to ask them for the bones as you need them for your stock. Cut into large
chunks and set to one side.

Clean the shellfish. Put your shellfish in a hot pan with a little olive oil, a splash
of white wine and seasoning. Keep over the heat for about five minutes, until
they are open. Strain and keep the juices for the stock.

Dice the onions, carrots and celery. Cook gently in a large pan. To this add the chopped tomatoes as well as the juice from the tin. Now add the white wine, fish stock, shellfish juices and saffron. This will smell amazing by now and should be of a thick, dense consistency. Bring this to the boil and simmer for ten minutes.

Add the pieces of fish and cook – really not for long at all! Then add the shellfish and season with salt, pepper, fresh chopped basil and parsley.

Works as a hearty starter or as a meal in itself.

Photo by Sarah Poli

Panna Cotta

From Lino and Sarah Poli

Trina says...

I just can't get enough of the Poli's Panna Cotta. I've been eating it for years, as Sarah and Lino used to have it on the menu of their Italian restaurant Firenze (which evolved into the Lighthouse), which we used to frequent way before we moved to Kibworth. So you can imagine how excited I was to be given the recipe. It turns out that Panna Cotta's subtle sophistication belies the ease of creation. Although Lino, yours does have that certain "un certo non so che!" I am therefore very pleased to tell you that they decided to keep it on the Lighthouse 'Bill of Fare'.

A little word of caution from someone who's easily distracted – try not to let the cream on the side of the pan burn. And when turning them out, don't leave them in the hot water too long – like I did!

1 litre of double cream
60g caster sugar
2 leaves of gelatine
1 vanilla pod or essence

Allow the gelatine to soak in cold water until it is soft.

Pour the cream into a pan with the sugar and vanilla and bring to the boil.

Drain the gelatine.

Once the cream mixture has come to the boil, remove from the heat and stir in the gelatine.

Allow this mix to cool and pour into your moulds. You'll need about 6 x 150ml. Mini pudding moulds are ideal.

Put the moulds in the fridge and chill until they are set.

To serve

Suspend the moulds in a bowl of hot water for just a moment in order to release the Panna Cotta from the sides. You may need to run a knife around it too, then 'shake' out of the mould onto a plate.

Panna Cotta may be accompanied by various scrummy things – a compote of summer fruits, strawberries in caramel, raspberry coulis, oranges in Grand Marnier, or a dark chocolate sauce. Try these or make it up as you go along – any way it is delicious. There are some that say that it is sacrilege to serve it any way other than in its purest form, totally nude!

The true art is in the Panna Cotta and getting exactly right the quantity of gelatine. If yours is too firm you can melt it down over a bain marie, add more cream and try again. If it is too soft then try scooping it into pretty presentation glasses and layer it with fruit!

DEBBIE'S MOST WONDERFUL BOOKSHOP

Trina says...

Debbie James came to Leicestershire because of her previous job in the music industry. However, in 2009 Debbie decided it was time to 'live the dream' she'd always had of owning a bookshop. She spotted an empty shop on Kibworth Beauchamp High Street and has never looked back.

Debbie's enthusiasm for literature and the village is endless, and winning the regional round of the Independent Bookseller of the Year Award after just a few years in business is testament to her dedication and enthusiasm. What a wonderful asset The Bookshop is to the High Street.

Debbie's Cheese Scone recipe is one of her mum's. They are delicious warm with a thick slick of butter.

Debbie's Mum's Cheese Scones

From Mrs. James

Mrs. James says...

Freshly-baked scones should be pulled gently apart with fingers. Cutting spoils the texture and makes them doughy. As scones stale quickly it is preferable to make and eat them on the same day.
Makes 9-10 scones

1/2 lb self-raising flour
1 level teaspoon dry mustard
1/2 level teaspoon salt
pinch of cayenne pepper
2 oz cheddar cheese – very finely-grated
2 oz English or Welsh butter
1/4 pint milk
extra milk for brushing

Sift flour, dry mustard, salt and cayenne pepper into bowl. Rub in butter finely. Mix in cheddar cheese

Add milk all at once. Mix to soft, but not sticky dough with knife. Turn onto lightly-floured board. Knead quickly until smooth.

Roll out to about 1/2 inch thickness. Cut into 9 or 10 rounds with 2 1/2 inch biscuit cutter.

Transfer to buttered baking tray. Brush tops with milk. Bake towards top of hot oven (gas mark 8) for 7-10 minutes, or until well risen and golden brown.

Cool on a wire rack.

Winter in Kibworth

SAMANTHA SCOTT – THE CONFIDENT COOK

Samantha Scott who has lived in Kibworth Beauchamp since 2003 runs The Confident Cook Ltd. Sam started the company in 2011 following a varied career that encompassed corporate entertaining, hotel management and crew catering for pop bands. Her work has taken her all around the UK and Europe working for multinational organisations and international artists.

Originally The Confident Cook Ltd was a local cookery school teaching clients in their own homes, but more recently the company has become heavily involved in artist and crew catering for the music industry, with contracts throughout the UK, most notably the Royal Albert Hall.

Locally, Sam organises the very popular annual Kibworth Food Festival and provides bespoke outdoor catering for companies in South East Leicestershire.

Chicken and Leek Pie

From Sam Scott

Sam says...

A delicious and simple traditional dish, enjoy with seasonal vegetables. The pie filling can be made a day or two in advance, but allow 45–50 minutes cooking time if being cooked from chilled. It serves six people.

2 blocks of pre prepared puff pastry
350g skinless and boneless chicken – meat from legs and thighs cut into bite sized pieces
2 medium leeks – finely sliced
110g baby button mushrooms – cut into quarters
half a cup of frozen peas
half a cup of sweetcorn
2 pints white sauce – shop packet does fine
a third bottle white wine
1 tablespoon flat leaf parsley – roughly chopped
2 teaspoons fresh thyme
1 garlic clove – crushed
3 tablespoons olive oil
50g butter
salt and pepper
4 drops tabasco sauce
1 tablespoon flour
2 medium eggs – beaten

Preheat oven to 200°c (fan 180°c) or Gas mark 6. You will need a deep sided oven proof dish approximately 13cm x 8cm or equivalent.

Gently heat the oil and butter in a large non-stick saucepan. Add the leeks and cook for a few minutes until softened. Stir in the garlic and thyme then add salt and pepper to taste. Pour in the white wine, stir, and simmer until the liquid has reduced by half.

Place the chicken in the pan and mix well. Leave to cook for a couple of minutes before stirring again. This prevents the chicken from breaking up and allows it to seal in the pan. When the chicken has turned white in colour, mix in the rest of the

vegetables and cook for five minutes. Pour over the white sauce, season with more salt and pepper and add the tabasco (this is optional).

Leave to cook on a gentle heat for 20 minutes, stirring occasionally to make sure the white sauce doesn't burn on the bottom of the pan. Place the pie mix in your selected dish and leave to one side.

Measure the size of your dish before rolling out your pastry. This will give you an idea of how big your pie lid needs to be. Roll the pastry on a lightly-floured surface. Make sure you roll it a little bigger than needed to give you an overhang on the dish. Brush the edge of the pie dish with the beaten egg before placing the pastry on top of the pie. Seal the pastry to the dish by pressing down around the pie edge with your fingers.

Create your own design with the left over pastry (you could cut out the words PIE or create leaves, etc.) and fix it to the top of the pie crust with the beaten egg. Brush all the pastry with remaining egg mix and pierce a hole in the top to allow any steam to escape while cooking.

Sit on a baking tray and place in the oven for 25–30 minutes, until the pastry is puffed up and nicely golden. Cut the excess pastry off the pie lid before serving!

Stuffed Mediterranean Pork Loin

From Sam Scott

1 large pork fillet – about 500g
200g sun blush tomatoes – chopped
20 slices Parma or Serrano ham
600g mozzarella – sliced
salt and black pepper to taste
large handful of baby spinach leaves
olive oil

Preheat oven to 200°c (fan 180°c) or Gas mark 6.

Lay the pork fillet on a chopping board and cut away any white sinew attached to the outside. Cut through the centre of fillet, being careful only to cut halfway through the meat.

Lay the cut fillet in between two large pieces of cling film – like a sandwich! Using a rolling pin or the smooth flat side of a meat mallet, gently beat the fillet out until it is about twice its original size. Remove the top layer of cling film.

Cover the fillet with a layer of spinach leaves, then spoon over the chopped tomatoes and cover with the mozzarella slices.

Using the bottom piece of cling film to help, roll the pork up lengthways making sure that all the ingredients are trapped inside. Place the rolled fillet to one side.

Arrange the slices of ham side-by-side across the work surface so that they slightly overlap each other. Place the rolled fillet across the centre of the ham layer. Fold each piece of ham across the fillet so that they completely cover the pork. Tuck in at either end to seal the meat. Tie string around each end and the middle to secure.

Place the fillet into a shallow roasting tin and cook for between 30 and 40 minutes until the ham has gone a golden colour.

Remove from the oven. Test the meat with a sharp knife. If the juices run clear the meat is cooked. Leave the pork in the tin, and cover with foil. Allow the meat to rest for ten minutes before carving into diagonal slices approximately 3cm across and serving.

Serve with seasonal steamed vegetables and a sauce or gravy of your choice.

Baked Cod with Herb Crust and Tartare Sauce

From Sam Scott

_____ Sam says... _____

*A delicious and tasty supper dish. We suggest serving with a green
leaf salad and/or sautéed potatoes. It serves four.*

For The Cod
4 x 225g thick cod fillets – skinned
olive oil – for drizzling and greasing
75g fresh white breadcrumbs
zest of 1 lemon – finely grated
4 tablespoons chopped fresh parsley
1 tablespoon chopped fresh chives
1 fat garlic clove – finely chopped
25g butter – melted

For the Tartare Sauce
1 egg yolk
1 1/2 teaspoons white wine vinegar
1 1/2 teaspoons English mustard
salt
150ml sunflower oil
2 teaspoons each of green olives, gherkins and capers – finely chopped
2 teaspoons each of fresh chives and curly parsley – finely chopped

Preheat oven to 220°c (fan 200°c) or Gas mark 8.
Season the cod on both sides and lay skinned-side up on a well-oiled baking tray.

Place the breadcrumbs, lemon zest, parsley, chives, garlic and seasoning into a bowl. Add the butter and mix well with a fork. Divide the breadcrumb mixture between the fillets and press on top of each piece in a thick, even layer. Drizzle over a little oil and bake for 10-12 minutes, or until the crust is crisp and lightly golden and the fish is cooked through. Lift onto warm plates and serve.

For the Tartare Sauce

Put the egg yolk, vinegar, mustard and 1/4 teaspoon salt into a food processor and blend briefly. With the machine running, add the oil in a steady stream to make a thick mayonnaise.

Transfer to a small bowl and stir in the other ingredients.

Chill in the fridge whilst fish is prepared and cooked.

Sam's Chocolate Mousse

From Sam Scott

Sam says...

A delicious and easy to make chocolate mousse that just melts in the mouth. Makes six.

320g quality dark eating chocolate – 70% cocoa solids
5g icing sugar
coffee mix – 1 teaspoon of instant coffee to 5 teaspoons boiling water
6 eggs
small punnet of raspberries
grated white chocolate and flaked milk chocolate for presentation

Break the chocolate into small pieces and put them in a roomy bowl set over a pan with a centimetre of barely simmering water in, to melt slowly. Set to one side.

Separate the eggs, placing the whites into a large bowl. Whisk the egg whites until they make soft peaks. Fold in the icing sugar.

In a separate bowl, beat the yolks with a fork.

Stir the coffee into the cooled melted chocolate, then add the eggs yolks. Ensure the chocolate is cool enough so as not to cook the egg.

Cut and fold half the egg whites into the chocolate. Repeat with the other half until all the egg white is used up.

Place a few raspberries (as many as you wish) into the bottom of six glasses. Pour the chocolate mixture over the raspberries so that each glass is 2/3 filled. Refrigerate for four hours to set. Before serving, cover the top of the mousse with grated white chocolate and finish with a light dusting of the flaked milk chocolate.

INDEX